Scary Snakes

by Monica Hughes

Consultant: Mitch Cronick

BEARPORT
PUBLISHING COMPANY, INC.
New York, New York

Credits

t=top, b=bottom, c=center, l=left, r=right, OFC=outside front cover
Alamy: 18–19. Corbis: 13. FLPA: 16, 17, 22b.
Superstock: 7, 9, 14, 15, 22t, 22c, 23c, 23b.
ticktock photography: 4, 5, 6, 11, 12, 20, 21, 23t.

Library of Congress Cataloging-in-Publication Data

Hughes, Monica.

Scary snakes / by Monica Hughes.

p. cm. — (I love reading)

Includes index.

ISBN 1-59716-154-3 (lib. bdg.) — ISBN 1-59716-180-2 (pbk.)

1. Snakes — Juvenile literature. I. Title. II. Series.

QL666.O6H86 2006

597.96 — dc22

2005030624

For more information, write to Bearport Publishing Company, Inc., 101 Fifth Avenue, Suite 6R, New York, New York 10003.
Printed in the United States of America.

10 9 8 7 6 5 4 3 2

CONTENTS

Meet some snakes

Snakes have scaly skin.

They **shed** their skin as they grow.

Scaly skin

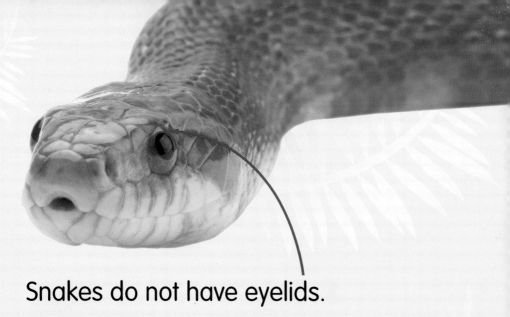

Snakes do not have eyelids.

They sleep with their eyes open.

Snakes have a
tongue shaped
like a "Y."

Snake babies

Some snakes lay eggs.

They lay eggs in nests made of leaves.

Baby snakes **hatch** from the eggs.

Corn snake

Some snakes do not lay eggs.

They give birth to live baby snakes.

Anaconda

King cobra

The king cobra is the biggest **poisonous** snake.

It can be 16 feet (5m) long.

The king cobra spits poison at its **prey**.

It eats birds, rats, and other snakes.

The king cobra lays eggs in a nest of leaves.

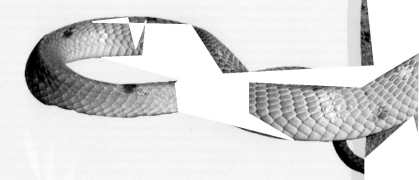

Ball python

This snake eats rats and gerbils.

It wraps its body around the prey.

Then it squeezes the prey to death.

The ball python lays eggs in a **burrow**.

Rattlesnake

Rattlesnakes live in hot deserts.

They eat rats and mice.

Rattlesnakes bite their prey with poisonous **fangs**.

They have hard scales on their tails that rattle.

Rattlesnakes give birth to live baby snakes.

13

Anaconda

The anaconda eats pigs and deer.

It wraps its body around the prey.

Then it squeezes the prey to death.

Emerald tree boa

Emerald tree boas live in rain forests.

They eat birds and mice.

They give birth to live baby snakes.

The baby snakes can be many different colors.

Adder

Adders are poisonous.

They eat rats and lizards.

They chase their prey or **ambush** it.

Adders give birth to 20 live
baby snakes at once.

Corn snake

Corn snakes live in trees and under rocks.

Corn snakes are not scary.

They are not poisonous.

They make good pets.

Corn snakes eat rats and mice.

They lay their eggs in old leaves.

21

Glossary

ambush (AM-bush)
to hide and then attack
someone or something

burrow (BUR-oh)
a tunnel or hole in
the ground

fangs (FANGZ)
long, sharp teeth

hatch (HACH) to come out of an egg

poisonous (POI-zuhn-uss) something that can kill or hurt animals or plants

prey (PRAY) an animal that is hunted for food

shed (SHED) to let something fall off

Index

Learn More

Parsons, Alexandra. *Amazing Snakes.* New York: Knopf Books for Young Readers (1990).

Pringle, Laurence. *Snakes! Strange and Wonderful.* Honesdale, PA: Boyds Mills Press (2004).

http://yahooligans.yahoo.com/content/animals/reptiles/

www.kidsplanet.org/factsheets/snakes.html